LEGO LEGENDS OF CHIMA

HEROES' QUEST

WRITTEN BY
HEATHER SEABROOK

LONDON, NEW YORK, MUNICH,
MELBOURNE, and DELHI

DK LONDON
Senior Editor Sadie Smith
Pre-Production Producer Marc Staples
Producer Louise Minihane
Managing Editor Elizabeth Dowsett
Design Manager Ron Stobbart
Publishing Manager Julie Ferris
Publishing Director Simon Beecroft

DK DELHI
Assistant Editor Gaurav Joshi
Assistant Art Editor Pranika Jain
Art Editor Divya Jain
Deputy Managing Editor Chitra Subramanyam
Deputy Managing Art Editor Neha Ahuja
DTP Designer Umesh Singh Rawat
Senior DTP Designer Jagtar Singh
Pre-Production Manager Sunil Sharma

Reading Consultant
Linda B. Gambrell, Ph.D.

First American Edition, 2014
10 9 8 7 6 5 4 3 2 1
Published in the United States by DK Publishing
345 Hudson Street, New York, New York 10014

LEGO, the LEGO logo, the Brick and Knob configurations, the Minifigure,
and LEGENDS OF CHIMA are trademarks of the LEGO Group.
© 2014 The LEGO Group
Produced by Dorling Kindersley under license from the LEGO Group.

001–256566–Apr/14

DK books are available at special discounts when purchased in bulk for sales promotions,
premiums, fund-raising, or educational use.
For details, contact:
DK Publishing Special Markets
345 Hudson Street, New York, New York 10014
SpecialSales@dk.com

A catalog record for this book is available
from the Library of Congress.

ISBN: 978-1-4654-1982-8 (Paperback)
ISBN: 978-1-4654-1981-1 (Hardback)

Color reproduction by Alta Image
Printed and bound in China by South China

Discover more at
www.dk.com
www.LEGO.com

Contents

Trouble in Chima™!

The beautiful kingdom of Chima™ is home to special animal tribes who can walk and talk like people. They get their powers from a Sacred Pool full of an energy source called CHI.

But there is trouble in the land of Chima, and the tribes are worried. The water has stopped flowing from Mount Cavora and the Sacred Pool has dried up. The tribes believe that the mythical creatures called Legend Beasts can restart the waterfalls and save Chima.

The Legend Beasts are animals who did not drink from the Sacred Pool. They walk on four legs and are like normal animals, but giant in size.

Black smoke

Mountain of Life
Mount Cavora was once beautiful and green. Its waterfalls were full of energy-rich CHI.

Band of Heroes

The tribes of Chima used to fight each other over CHI. Now that somebody is trying to take it away from them, they realize that they must join together.

The tribes have chosen their bravest animals to form a band of heroes.

They include Eris the Eagle, Gorzan the Gorilla, Rogon the Rhino, Laval the Lion, Cragger the Crocodile, and Worriz the Wolf.

Together they must travel through the dangerous Outlands jungle in order to find the Legend Beasts.

Laval the Lion

Laval is the son of King LaGravis. He loves to have fun and is eager for adventure. Laval is also headstrong and has a lot to learn. One day he will lead the Lion Tribe and rule over the land of Chima.

Laval thinks he is ready to face the crisis in Chima. He wants to prove to his father that he can be responsible and brave. The journey into the Outlands will be full of danger, but Laval knows that the heroes must be fearless and find the mysterious Legend Beasts.

Cragger the Crocodile

Cragger is very stubborn and does not like to follow rules. He thinks he knows more than everyone else. Above all he likes to win!

Cragger was once Laval's best friend, but now they are enemies. They had a big fight after Cragger used CHI when he was not allowed. Secretly, Cragger misses his friendship with Laval.

Vengious Sword

Now that Chima is in trouble Cragger must work with Laval to bring back CHI to the Sacred Pool. Maybe this is the chance for them to become friends once again.

Eris the Eagle

Eris is from the Eagle Tribe and is the daughter of one of the many ruling Eagles. She is very clever and loves adventures and puzzles.

Eris is a good friend and always helps others. She is very fond of Rogon the Rhino. In battle, Eris uses her brains to figure out a peaceful way to win rather than fighting. Eris is a very useful member of the brave team of heroes.

Worriz the Wolf

Worriz is from the Wolf Tribe. He is ruthless and cunning, and always puts himself and his Tribe first.

The Wolves do not get along with the other Tribes, but they must send one of their own to help save Chima. Worriz has been chosen to join the band of heroes. He will travel with the other heroes through the scary Outlands to find the Legend Beasts.

Even though Worriz has never met the Wolf Legend Beast, he loves him. He is determined to find the beast, no matter what it takes.

*Derimous
Sword*

Rogon the Rhino

Rogon, like the rest of the Rhino Tribe, can be a little stupid. He likes to have fun and is a bit of a party animal.

Rogon does not really understand what the mission is about and why they have to go. But he is coming along for the fun!

Rock Flinger
Rogon's massive truck can hurl rocks at enemies at very high speeds.

However, Rogon is very strong and is good to have on your side—especially when he uses his powerful Rammer Slammer against the enemy!

Gorzan the Gorilla

Gorzan is very laidback and sensitive, like most Gorillas. He cares about little things like flowers and insects. Even while fighting he cannot stop worrying about the poor little flowers that he may have stepped on.

Banana Buster

Gorzan's favorite weapon is the Banana Buster. It has a giant fist that pops out on a spring.

Gorzan is a strong and powerful fighter. When he gets angry, he can be a very scary opponent for even the strongest of the Outland Tribes.

Lavertus the Lion

Lavertus is an outlaw of the Lion Tribe. He was banished to live in the Outlands after an argument with King LaGravis.

Lavertus lives in a place called the "Lair"—a home he has built himself. He flies a special helicopter vehicle called the WindShadow. He is very good at building things!

Lavertus welcomes the heroes on their arrival in the Outlands and offers to help them on their mission.

He uses special tools to improve their weapons, and builds new armor for everyone. The heroes have made an important new friend.

Rotor blade

The Spider Tribe

The Spider Tribe lives in the Outlands. They are the smartest of all the Outland Tribes.

The spiders are very good at building webs and traps. They can use the webs to capture their enemies.

Once, the spiders even used their sticky webs to block the waterfalls of Mount Cavora.

The tribe is ruled over by Spinlyn, the very vain spider queen. She looks hideous to every creature except other spiders. The queen has many spider soldiers at her service.

Web trap

The spiders are masters at weaving sticky webs. Once trapped, the enemies have little hope of escaping.

The Arachnaught

The Arachnaught is a big battle vehicle that walks on eight mechanical spider legs. It shoots out fully formed webs as well as streams of webbing. The webs trap enemies and tangle them up, and the streams of webbing knock them off their feet.

The Arachnaught looks scary with its glowing red eyes and sharp spider fangs. It even has a weapons holder underneath its body. The Arachnaught's powerful stomping front legs are a match for even the strongest and biggest hero.

Sharp claws

Sting

Selfish king

King Scorm has plans for
world domination. He does
not care about the other
Outland Tribes and is
just using them.

The Scorpion Tribe

The Scorpions are the most powerful of the Outland Tribes. Scorpions come in three ranks: the king, Stompers, and Scrappers. Stompers are big, black scorpions who walk on six legs. The king wears gold armor and walks on two legs. Scrappers are small foot soldiers.

The Scorpions use their tails for clubbing and stinging. Stompers can even shoot poison from their tails!

The scorpion king is named Scorm. He is power-hungry and gets angry very easily. Scorm wants all of the CHI for himself.

Scorpion Stinger

The Scorpion Assault Vehicle is a mean machine that attacks with its massive claws and pincers. Three wheels help keep it balanced so that it does not topple over.

The Stinger's tail jabs up and down to try and sting its enemies. The tail also shoots toxic "VenomBalls." Powerful pincers on the mouth crush anything in their way.

The Scorpion pilots sit in the cockpit
and steer the Stinger into battle. The
VenomBalls are loaded on the side,
ready to be used against the enemy.

VenomBall

CHI

The Bat Tribe

The Bat Tribe is the weakest and most stupid of all the Outland Tribes. Their strength lies in numbers—there are hundreds of them!

The Bat Tribe is the only Outland Tribe that can fly. They use compact aircraft called Bat Flyers to penetrate the energy field around Mount Cavora. The Bat Flyers blow out menacing black smoke that surrounds Mount Cavora.

Bommerommer is the leader of the tribe. He will do whatever the Scorpions and Spiders tell him. His trusted assistants are Braptor and Blista. Braptor is the pilot of a powerful vehicle called the Wingstriker.

Gorilla Legend Beast

The Gorilla Legend Beast is bigger and stronger than Gorzan and his tribe. He is also gentle and loves having fun, just like Gorzan.

The band of heroes find the Gorilla Legend Beast first. They are relieved, but they have a difficult task ahead.

They have to first rescue him from the evil Spider tribe. He is caught in a huge spider web in the Spider canyon. The heroes disguise Rogon's truck as a big fly to distract the Spiders and free the trapped Beast.

Now the heroes have hope. They can continue their quest to find the other Legend Beasts.

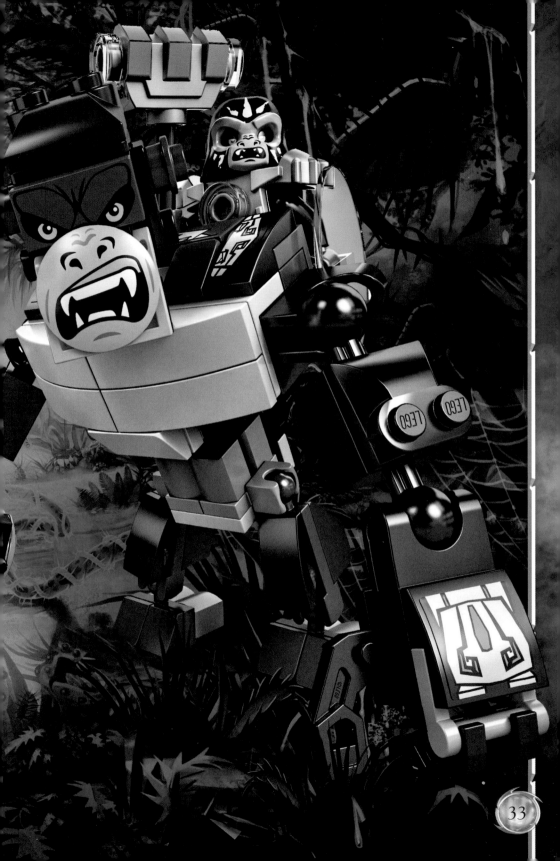

Eagle Legend Beast

The Eagle Legend Beast is a powerful bird of prey. She has huge wings, sharp talons, and a strong beak. The Beast is very protective of her two eggs.

But, she is upset. The evil Outland Tribes have captured her eggs and trapped them on the Seesaw Rock. If the heroes are not careful, the eggs could slide off the slab and fall onto the jagged rocks below!

Eris rides on the back of the mighty Eagle Beast to try and reach the eggs. Lavertus the Lion also comes to help on his WindShadow helicopter.

Talons

Eris puts her battle tactics to use.
Together with the band of heroes,
she finally manages to save the eggs.

Crocodile Legend Beast

The Crocodile Legend Beast is a strong swimmer and feels most at home in the water.

Like the other Legend Beasts, he is very big. Watch out for his shiny, white teeth—they are really sharp!

Scales

The Crocodile Beast likes Cragger. He lets him sit on his back and ride him across land or water. It is very useful when the heroes fall into a flooded canyon! Courageous Cragger rescues his friends by swimming out to them on the Crocodile Beast.

Strong jaws

Wolf Legend Beast

The Wolf Tribe gives Worriz the special "Mother Tooth" charm to take on the quest. It will help Worriz find the Legend Beast. His tribe believes that the tooth belongs to the Wolf Beast. Worriz has a special connection with the Beast and is the only one who can understand his howl.

The Wolf Beast is trapped in the Scorpion cave. He has been put in a trance by Scorpion poison. Worriz uses the "Mother Tooth" to wake the Legend Beast from his trance.

The fierce Wolf Beast is very tough and once he is out of the trance, he easily escapes from the Scorpion cave.

Lion Legend Beast

The strong and noble Lion is the last of the Legend Beasts to be found. He is big and powerful with a thick brown mane and sharp claws. Laval decides to rescue him all by himself.

The Beast is trapped across a pool of water. Just like Laval, the Legend Beast is scared of water. He will not swim across the pool.

Laval overcomes his fear. He swims through the pool and helps the Legend Beast to swim back with him.

Raw power
The Lion Legend Beast relies on his strong jaws and strength to deal with enemies.

Return to Chima

Victory! The heroes have finally found the Legend Beasts and defeated the Outland Tribes. Evil King Scorm vows to fight again when he gets more CHI. However, Laval gives Scorm the last orb of CHI. He explains that CHI must always be shared. The heroes have survived the dangers of the Outlands.

They return home to Chima, where the Legend Beasts magically fly into the waterfall caves of Mount Cavora. The water starts to flow again and CHI is restored to the Sacred Pool. The land of Chima and the animal tribes are saved!

Lion Temple

Quiz

1. What is the name of the land that the animal tribes live in?

2. Where can you find the magical energy source known as CHI?

3. Who are the Band of Heroes looking for in the Outlands?

4. Who is Laval's father?

5. Who is Eris fond of?

6. What is Rogon's massive rock-filled truck called?

7. Which of the Outland Tribes is the smartest?

8. How do the spiders capture
   their enemies?

9. How many wheels does the
   Scorpion Assault Vehicle have?

10. What is the Lion Legend
    Beast scared of?

Answers on
page 47

Glossary

determined
wanting to
do something
very much

domination
have power or
control over
someone or
something

headstrong
someone who
only does what
they want to do

menacing
a person or
thing likely
to cause harm

mythical
existing only
in stories

penetrate
to move into
or through

responsible
to have control
or be in charge

tactics
plan of attack

trance
a dreamy state
where a person
does not know
what is going
on around them

vain
obsessed with your
own appearance

Index

Answers to the quiz on pages 44 and 45:
1. Chima 2. In the Sacred Pool 3. The Legend Beasts
4. King LaGravis 5. Rogon the Rhino 6. Rock Flinger
7. The Spiders 8. With their webs 9. Three 10. Water

DK

Here are some other DK Readers you might enjoy.

Level 3

LEGO® *Star Wars*™: Revenge of the Sith
The Jedi must save the galaxy from the Sith!
Will Anakin fall to the dark side?

LEGO® Chima™: The Race for CHI
Jump into battle with the animal tribes as they
fight to get their claws on the CHI!

Shark Reef
Blanche, Ash, Harry, and Moby are the sharks who live
on the reef. Be entertained by their shark visitors that
come passing through.

Level 4

Star Wars™: Darth Maul Sith Apprentice
Get ready to enter the dark side and discover everything
about the evil Darth Maul—if you dare!

Dinosaur Detectives
Track dinosaurs with the earliest fossil hunters and modern-
day geologists! Read about their amazing discoveries!

Earthquakes and Other Natural Disasters
Earthquakes, volcanoes, fires, and floods—discover
the awesome power of nature unleashed!